Teach Me...™
French
and
More French

by Judy Mahoney

Teach Me French and More French
Two books in one, twice the fun!
Over 40 songs to sing and learn French

The classic coloring books *Teach Me French* and *Teach Me More French* are now combined into a new bind up edition. This new edition includes the original coloring pages from both titles with a 60 minute audio CD. *Teach Me French and More French* also features eight new pages of expanded vocabulary and activities.

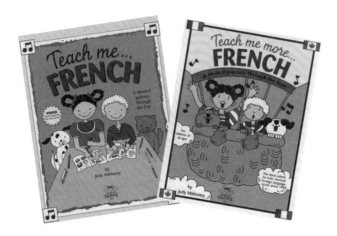

Our mission at Teach Me Tapes is to enrich children through language learning. The **Teach Me**... series of books offers an engaging approach to language acquisition by using familiar children's songs and providing an audio to sing and learn. Studies show that a child's early exposure to new languages and cultures enhances learning skills and promotes a better appreciation of our multicultural world. What better gift to offer our youth than the tools and ideas to understand the world we live in?

Many French-speaking countries, and the regions within them, have their own dialects of the language. All French nouns have a gender; therefore, the article preceding the noun indicates masculine or feminine, as well as singular or plural. We believe it is important for children to listen, speak, read and write the language to enhance their learning experience.

Today's "global children" hold tomorrow's world in their hands!

Teach Me French & More French
Bind Up Edition
Book with CD
ISBN: 978-1-59972-601-4
Library of Congress Control Number: 2009901068

Copyright © 2009 Teach Me Tapes, Inc.
6016 Blue Circle Drive
Minnetonka, MN 55343-9104
1-800-456-4656
www.teachmetapes.com

Translations are not literal.
Printed in the United States of America
10 9 8 7 6 5 4 3 2

Teach me...
FRENCH

A Musical
Journey
Through
the Day

by
Judy Mahoney

Teach Me...™
www.teachmetapes.com

 Plus nous sommes ensemble

Plus nous sommes ensemble, ensemble, ensemble
Plus nous sommes ensemble, plus heureux nous serons
Parce que tes amis sont mes amis, et mes amis sont tes amis
Plus nous sommes ensemble, plus heureux nous serons.

Bonjour. Je m'appelle Marie.
Comment t'appelles-tu?
Voici ma famille.

Mon père

Ma mère

Moi

Mon frère

Mon chat

Il s'appelle Minou. Il est gris.

Mon Chien

Il s'appelle Médor. Il est noir et blanc.

Et voici ma maison. Elle a un toit marron et un jardin avec des fleurs jaunes.

Ma chambre est bleue. Il est sept heures.
Réveille-toi! Réveille-toi!

 **Alouette**

Alouette, gentille alouette
Alouette, je te plumerai.
Je te plumerai le bec,
Je te plumerai le bec,
Et le bec, alouette.

 Frère Jacques

Frère Jacques, Frère Jacques,
Dormez-vous? Dormez-vous?
Sonnez les matines,
Sonnez les matines,
Ding, dang, dong!
Ding, dang, dong!

4 QUATRE

Aujourd'hui c'est lundi. Connais-tu les jours de la semaine?

LUNDI

MARDI

MERCREDI

JEUDI

VENDREDI

SAMEDI

DIMANCHE

♪ **Tête, épaules, genoux et pieds**

Tête, épaules, genoux et pieds, genoux et pieds *répète*
J'ai deux yeux, un nez, une bouche et deux oreilles,
Tête, épaules, genoux et pieds, genoux et pieds.

Il fait mauvais. Il pleut. Je ne peux pas me promener aujourd'hui.

 Pluie, pluie va-t-en

Pluie, pluie va-t-en
Reviens un autre jour
Petit Jean veut jouer
Pluie, pluie va-t-en.

 Les arcs en ciel

Parfois bleu et parfois vert
Les couleurs les plus jolies
Que j'ai jamais vues
Rose et mauve, jaune oui...
J'aime me balancer
Sous ces arcs en ciel.

Voici mon école. Je dis,«Bonjour, maîtresse».
Je répète mes nombres et mon alphabet.

1 2 3 4 5
6 7 8 9 10

A B
C D E F G H
I J K L M N
O P Q R S T
U V W X Y Z

♪ Marie avait un p'tit agneau

Marie avait un p'tit agneau
D'une teinte de neige pure
Et n'importe où Marie flânait
L'agneau suivait pour sûr.

♪ Un Eléphant

Deux éléphants
Allaient jouer
Sur une toile
D'araignée
Ils s'amusaient
Tellement bien
Qu'ils appelaient
Un autre, viens!

♪ Ainsi font

Ainsi font, font, font
Les petites marionnettes
Ainsi font, font, font
Trois p'tits tours
Et puis s'en vont.

Après l'école, nous allons en voiture à la maison.

 Les roues de la voiture

Les roues de la voiture tournent et tournent,
Tournent et tournent, tournent et tournent,
Les roues de la voiture tournent et tournent,
Partout dans la ville.

Le klaxon de la voiture fait bip bip bip,
Bip bip bip, bip bip bip,
Le klaxon de la voiture fait bip bip bip,
Partout dans la ville.

Les enfants dans la voiture disent «allons manger»,
«Allons manger», «allons manger»,
Les enfants dans la voiture disent «allons manger»,
Partout dans la ville.

C'est l'heure du déjeuner. Après le déjeuner, c'est la sieste.

 **Dodo gentil bébé**

Dodo gentil bébé
Dors en silence.
Papa est parti
T'acheter un canari.
Si ce canari ne chante pas,
Papa t'achètera
Une bague en diamant.
Si ce diamant ne brille pas,
Papa t'achètera
Un beau miroir doré.
Si ce miroir se brise
Papa t'achètera
Une jolie petite chèvre.

 **Sur le pont d'Avignon**

Sur le pont d'Avignon
L'on y danse, l'on y danse,
Sur le pont d'Avignon
L'on y danse tout en rond.

 Jean et Jeanne

Jean et Jeanne sur la montagne
Un seau d'eau douce cherchèrent;
Jean tomba, la tête se cassa,
Jeanne culbuta derrière.

Après la sieste, nous allons au parc. Je vois des canards. Je chante, je danse sur le pont avec mes amis.

 Six petits canards

Six petits canards que je connaissais
Des gros, des minces, des jolis aussi
Mais un petit canard avec une plume
Sur le dos, il guidait les autres avec
Son coin coin coin, coin coin coin,
Coin coin coin. *répète*

Y'a un rat

Y'a un rat, dans le grenier, j'entends
Le chat qui miaule. Y'a un rat,
Dans le grenier, j'entends le chat
Miauler. J'entends, j'entends,
J'entends le chat qui miaule.
J'entends, j'entends, j'entends
Le chat miauler.

J'ai faim. C'est l'heure du dîner.

 **Oh! Susanna**

J'arrive tout droit de l'Alabama, avec mon banjo sous le bras

Je vais comme ça vers la Louisiane, pour retrouver ma Susanna.

Oh! Susanna, ne pleure pas pour moi

J'arrive tout droit de l'Alabama, avec mon banjo sous le bras.

Il fait nuit. Vois-tu les 'étoiles? Bonne nuit, Maman. Bonne nuit, Papa. Je vous aime.

Bonsoir mes amis, bonsoir.

♪ **Ah! vous dirai-je Maman**

Ah! vous dirai-je Maman
Ce qui cause mon tourment?
Papa veut que je raisonne
Comme une grande personne
Moi, je dis que les bonbons
Valent mieux que la raison.

♪ **Fais dodo, Colas**

Fais dodo, Colas mon p'tit frère
Fais dodo, t'auras du lolo
Maman est en haut
Qui fait du gâteau
Papa est en bas
Qui fait du chocolat. *au refrain*

TRANSLATIONS

PAGE 1
The More We Get Together
The more we get together, together, together,
The more we get together the happier we'll be.
For your friends are my friends
And my friends are your friends
The more we get together the happier we'll be.

PAGE 2
Hello, my name is Marie. What is your name?
Here is my family. My mother, my father, my
brother and me.

PAGE 3
My cat. His name is Minou. He is grey.
My dog. His name is Médor. He is black and
white. Here is my house. It has a brown roof
and a garden with yellow flowers.

PAGE 4
My room is blue. It is seven o'clock.
Get up! Get up!

The Lark (Alouette)
Lark, oh lovely lark
Lark, I will pluck you now.
I will pluck your little beak *repeat*
And your beak, and your beak.

Are You Sleeping
Are you sleeping, are you sleeping?
Brother John, Brother John?
Morning bells are ringing
Morning bells are ringing
Ding dang dong! Ding dang dong!

PAGE 5
Today is Monday. Do you know the
days of the week? Monday, Tuesday,
Wednesday, Thursday, Friday,
Saturday, Sunday.

PAGE 6
I get dressed. I put on my shirt,
my pants, my shoes and my hat.
I eat breakfast. I like bread and
hot chocolate.

PAGE 7
Head, Shoulders, Knees and Toes
Head and shoulders, knees and toes,
Knees and toes, *repeat*
Eyes and ears and mouth and nose
Repeat first line

PAGE 8
The weather is bad. It is raining. I cannot go
for a walk today.

Rain, Rain, Go Away
Rain, rain, go away,
Come again another day,
Rain, rain, go away,
Little Johnny wants to play.

It's Raining, It's Pouring
It's raining, it's pouring
The old man is snoring
He bumped his head and went to bed
And couldn't get up in the morning.

Rainbows
Sometimes blue and sometimes green
Prettiest colors I've ever seen
Pink and purple, yellow-whee!
I love to ride those rainbows.
© Teach Me Tapes, Inc. 1985

PAGE 9
Here is my school. I say "Good morning,
teacher." I repeat my numbers and my
alphabet.

Page 10
Mary Had a Little Lamb
Mary had a little lamb
Its fleece was white as snow
Everywhere that Mary went
The lamb was sure to go.

One Elephant
One elephant went out to play
Upon a spider's web one day
He had such enormous fun that
He called for another elephant to come.

Ainsi Font
This is what they do
What the marionettes do
What they do
What they do, do, do
Three turns round and they're
Through, through, through.

PAGE 11

*After school, we drive in our car
to our house.*

The Wheels on the Car

The wheels on the car go round and round,
Round and round, round and round,
The wheels on the car go round and round
All around the town.

The horn on the car goes beep beep beep,
Beep beep beep, beep beep beep,
The horn on the car goes beep beep beep,
All around the town.

The children in the car go, "Let's have lunch,"
"Let's have lunch," "Let's have lunch,"
The children in the car go, "Let's have lunch,"
All around the town.

PAGE 12

It is lunch time. After lunch it is nap time.

Hush Little Baby

Hush little baby don't say a word
Papa's going to buy you a mockingbird
If that mockingbird don't sing
Papa's going to buy you a diamond ring
If that diamond ring turns brass
Papa's going to buy you a looking glass
If that looking glass falls down
You'll still be the sweetest little baby in town.

PAGE 13

*After our naps, we go to the park. I see
the ducks. I sing, I dance on the bridge
with my friends.*

On the Bridge of Avignon

On the bridge of Avignon
They're all dancing, they're all dancing
On the bridge of Avignon
They're all dancing round and round.

Jack and Jill

Jack and Jill went up the hill,
To fetch a pail of water;
Jack fell down and broke his crown,
And Jill came tumbling after.

Six Little Ducks

Six little ducks that I once knew,
Fat ones, skinny ones, fair ones too,
But the one little duck
With the feather on his back,
He led the others with his
Quack, quack, quack,
Quack, quack, quack,
Quack, quack, quack,
He led the others with his
Quack, quack, quack.

There's a Rat

There's a rat in the attic
I hear the cat who's meowing
There's a rat in the attic
I hear the cat meowing
I hear, I hear, I hear the cat who's meowing
I hear, I hear, I hear the cat meowing.

PAGE 14

I am hungry. It is dinner time.

Oh, Susanna

Well I come from Alabama
With my banjo on my knee
Going to Louisiana, my true love for to see.
Oh, Susanna, don't you cry for me
'Cause I come from Alabama
With my banjo on my knee.

PAGE 15

It's night time. Do you see the stars?

Twinkle, Twinkle

Twinkle, twinkle little star
How I wonder what you are
Up above the world so high
Like a diamond in the sky
Twinkle, twinkle little star
How I wonder what you are.
Note: "Ah! Vous dirai-je Maman" is a
traditional French song to the tune of
"Twinkle, Twinkle."

Go to Sleep, Colas

Go to sleep, Colas, my little brother
Go to sleep, and you'll have a treat
Mama is upstairs making cakes
Papa is downstairs making chocolate.

*Goodnight, Mommy. Goodnight, Daddy.
I love you.*

Note: Translations are not always literal.

Teach me more... FRENCH

by
Judy Mahoney

A Musical Journey Through the Year

Learn
French the
fun way!

Teach Me...™
www.teachmetapes.com

Marie: Bonjour. Je m'appelle Marie. Voilà mon frère. Il s'appelle Pierre. Nous avons un chien. Il s'appelle Médor. Nous avons un chat. Il s'appelle Minou. Suisnous pendant l'année.

Tu chanteras, je chanterai

Tu chanteras, je chanterai, nous chanterons ensemble
Tu chanteras, je chanterai, s'il fait beau ou mauvais.

Words and music by Ella Jenkins, ASCAP. Copyright 1966. Ell-Bern Publishing Co.

Pierre : C'est le printemps. Je plante un jardin de fleurs. Regarde mes fleurs rouges et jaunes.

Marie : Je plante des graines pour cultiver des légumes dans mon jardin. Cette année je cultiverai des tomates, des poivrons et des carottes.

Avoine, pois et persil poussent

Avoine, pois et persil poussent (*bis*)
Le sais-tu, le savez-vous
Si avoine, pois et persil poussent.

Le fermier plante les graines
Il respire, lève la tête
Tape des pieds, frappe des mains
Fait un tour admire son jardin.

Savez-vous planter les choux

Savez-vous planter les choux,
A la mode, à la mode,
Savez-vous planter les choux,
A la mode de chez nous.
On les plante avec le pied...
On les plante avec les mains...
On les plante avec le nez...

Allons au zoo

Maman nous emmène au zoo demain,
Zoo demain, zoo demain (*bis*)
Pour tout le matin.
Nous allons au zoo...o...o...
Pourquoi pas toi...toi...toi...
Viens avec moi...moi...moi
Nous allons au zoo...o...o....

Regarde tous les singes
Sauter dans les branches (*bis*)
Pour toute la journée.

Regarde dans l'eau
Nager les crocodiles (*bis*)
Pour toute la journée.

Marie: Aujourd'hui nous allons au zoo. Regarde le lion, la girafe et le singe.
Pierre: Mon animal préféré, c'est le crocodile.

Tingalayo

Tingalayo, viens petit âne viens.
Tingalayo, viens petit âne viens.
Mon âne vite, mon âne lent,
Mon âne viens et mon âne va t'en.
Mon âne vite, mon âne lent
Mon âne viens et mon âne va t'en.

Marie: Mon anniversaire est le 10 mai. Je ferai une fête avec mes amis. Ma mère me préparera un grand gâteau rond.

Pierre: D'accord, jouons à Jacques a dit.

Le jeu de Jacques a dit

Jacques dit ... "mettez la main droite sur la tête."
... "touchez le sol."
... "marchez."
... "applaudissez."
... "dites votre nom."
"Riez fort." ... "Jacques n'a rien dit!"

Pierre: Après le printemps vient l'été. Pendant l'été nous allons à la plage.

Marie: A la plage, je porte mon seau et ma pelle.

Marie et Pierre: Nous mettons nos maillots de bain et nous faisons de beaux châteaux dans le sable.

Marie: Médor, ne le casse pas!

Nageons, nageons

Nageons, nageons, dans la grande piscine
Quand il fait froid, quand il fait chaud
Des plongeons dans l'eau
Yeux fermés et sauter
Dans la grande piscine
Oh qu'il fait bon s'amuser
Toute la journée!

Rame, rame, rame

Rame, rame, rame donc
Vogue le canot
Joliment, joliment,
Joliment, joliment,
Attaquons les flots.

A la claire Fontaine

A la claire Fontaine
M'en allant promener
J'ai trouvé l'eau si belle
Que je m'y suis baignée.
Il y a longtemps que je t'aime
Jamais je ne t'oublierai.

5 CINQ

Marie: Après avoir nagé, nous mangeons notre pique-nique. Nous mangeons du pain, du fromage et des bananes. C'est délicieux!

Pierre: Oh non, regarde les fourmis!

Marie: Après le pique-nique, nous faisons une promenade.

Soleil se lève

Soleil, vois le soleil, soleil se lève je voudrais être chez moi (*bis*)
Bosse la nuit jusqu'au matin, soleil se lève je voudrais être chez moi
Charge les bananes jusqu'au matin, soleil...
Viens monsieur patron compter mes bananes, soleil... (*bis*)
Voilà six, voilà sept, voilà huit régimes, soleil... (*bis*)
Un beau régime de belles bananes, soleil... (*bis*)

Marie: Aujourd'hui nous allons au musée d'histoire naturelle.

Pierre: C'est mon endroit favori, parce qu'il y a beaucoup de dinosaures. Regarde le tricératops. Il a trois cornes sur la tête.

7 SEPT

Marie: Plus tard nous traversons la rue pour aller voir le musée d'art.

Pierre: J'aime regarder les taureaux dans les peintures de Goya. Je fais semblant d'être le matador.

Marie: Regarde les peintures de Van Gogh; les tournesols dans ses peintures ressemblent à ceux dans mon jardin.

Fille brune dans l'arène

Fille brune dans l'arène,
Tra-la-la-la-la (*bis*)
Elle a l'air d'une pêche
D'une prune, prune, prune.

2. Montre-moi un pas...
3. Enjambe l'océan...
4. Fais la locomotive...

Marie: Après l'été vient l'automne. Les feuilles deviennent dorées et violettes. Je ramasse les feuilles et les châtaignes.

Colchiques

Colchiques dans les prés fleurissent, fleurissent,
Colchiques dans les prés: c'est la fin de l'été.
La feuille d'automne emportée par le vent
En ronde monotone tombe en tourbillonnant.
Nuages dans le ciel s'étirent, s'étirent
Nuages dans le ciel s'étirent comme une aile.

Pierre: Avant de retourner à l'école, nous allons à la ferme de notre grand-papa. Nous donnons à manger aux vaches, aux poulets et aux cochons.

Marie: Mon grand-papa tond les agneaux. Plus tard, il nous promène dans un char avec nos cousins.

Agneau blanc

Agneau blanc as-tu un peu de laine?
Oui monsieur, oui monsieur,
Trois sacs pleins.
Un pour mon maître,
L'autre pour madame,
Un pour le garçon qui vit un peu plus loin.

A la ferme de grand-père

Ah allons tout de suite, *(bis)*
A la ferme de grand-père. *(bis)*
A la ferme de grand-père
Il y a une vache brune *(bis)*
La vache elle fait un son
Comme ça: Mou! Mou! *(bis)*

...Il y a un p'tit poulet rouge. *(Cot, cot)*

Père MacDonald

Père MacDonald a une ferme, E I E I O
Dans sa ferme il y a une vache, E I E I O
Avec meuh ici et meuh là-bas
Ici meuh, là-bas meuh
Partout des meuh, meuh
Père MacDonald a une ferme, E I E I O.

... Il y a une poule, un chat, un mouton.

Marie: Aujourd'hui nos parents nous emmènent à la fête des moissons. Les fermiers apportent leurs légumes pour un concours.

Pierre: Il y a beaucoup de manèges pour les enfants. J'aime monter sur le carrousel.

11 ONZE

Pierre: C'est Halloween. Je sculpte un visage dans mon potiron.

Marie: Ce soir je porterai un costume de "Chaperon Rouge" et Médor sera le loup. Pierre sera un "cowboy". Après, nous irons "trick or treating" avec nos amis.

Pierre: Après Halloween, vient le mois de novembre.

Cinq petits potirons

Cinq petits potirons assis dans le noir
Le premier a dit, "Mon Dieu, il est tard."
Le second a dit, "Sorcières dans le vent."
Le troisième a dit, "Ce n'est pas important."
Le quatrième dit, "Partons maintenant."
Le cinquième a dit, "Non, c'est amusant."
Hou...hou dit le vent, la lumière s'éteint
Et les potirons roulent dans le jardin.

Pierre : Regarde, la neige tombe. Allons jouer dans la neige. Nous tirons nos luges, allons sur la colline et glissons.

Marie : Plus tard nous faisons un bonhomme de neige. Il a des yeux de charbon, un nez de carotte et un chapeau melon. Il porte l'écharpe de ma mère.

Le bonhomme de neige

C'est un de mes amis
Le connais-tu aussi?
Il porte chapeau melon
Est froid comme un glaçon.

Deux yeux de charbon
Un nez de carotte jaune
Deux bras faits de bâton
Et un manteau de neige.

Devines-tu son nom?
Ecoute les informations.
Tu ne le verras jamais
Printemps, été, automne...
Qui est-ce?

Sainte nuit

Douce nuit, sainte nuit
Tout est calme, et sans bruits
L'enfant dort dans les bras de Marie
Et sa mère, le regarde sourire
Amour aux cheveux dorés
Jésus, nous est donné.

Marie: Ce sont les fêtes. Nous célébrons la fête de Noël.
Nous faisons des petits gâteaux et décorons la maison.
Pierre: Une nouvelle année commence en janvier. Nous
la célébrons par le Réveillon du Nouvel-An.

Ce n'est qu'un au revoir, mes frères

Ce n'est qu'un au revoir, mes frères, ce n'est qu'un au revoir
Ce n'est qu'un au revoir, mes frères, ce n'est qu'un au revoir.

Marie : En février nous fêtons le carnaval de Mardi Gras. C'est très amusant. J'aime attraper les bonbons lancés à la parade. Nous chantons et dansons avec nos amis.

Marie et Pierre : Maintenant nous connaissons les mois de l'année. Et toi? Janvier, février, mars, avril, mai, juin, juillet, août, septembre, octobre, novembre, décembre.

15 QUINZE

TRANSLATIONS

PAGE 1
You'll Sing a Song and I'll Sing a Song
You'll sing a song and I'll sing a song
And we'll sing a song together.
You'll sing a song and I'll sing a song,
In warm or wintry weather.
Words and music by Ella Jenkins. ASCAP
Copyright 1966. Ell-Bern Publishing Co.

MARIE: Hello. My name is Marie. This is my brother.
His name is Peter. We have a dog. His name is Medor.
We have a cat. His name is Minou. Follow us through the
year.

PAGE 2   MARCH
PETER: It is spring. I plant a flower garden. Look at my
red and yellow roses.
MARIE: I plant seeds to grow vegetables in my garden.
This year I will grow tomatoes, peppers and carrots.

Oats and Beans and Barley
Oats and beans and barley grow,
Oats and beans and barley grow.
Do you or I or anyone know
How oats and beans and barley grow?

First the farmer plants the seeds,
Stands up tall and takes his ease,
Stamps his feet and claps his hands
And turns around to view his land.

Savez-vous planter les choux
Do you know how to plant cabbage?
The way we do it at home:
We plant them with our foot...
We plant them with our hands...
We plant them with our nose...

PAGE 3   APRIL
MARIE: Today we go to the zoo. Look at the lion, the
giraffe and the monkey.
PETER: My favorite animal at the zoo is the crocodile.

Going to the Zoo
Mummy's taking us to the zoo tomorrow,
Zoo tomorrow, zoo tomorrow
Mummy's taking us to the zoo tomorrow,
We can stay all day.
We're going to the zoo, zoo, zoo.
How about you, you, you?
You can come too, too, too
We're going to the zoo, zoo, zoo.

Look at all the monkeys swinging in the trees...
Look at all the crocodiles swimming in the water...
Copyright 1961, 1969, 1981.
Cherry Lane Music Publishing Co. Inc.
All rights reserved. Used by permission.

Tingalayo
Tingalayo, come little donkey come.
Tingalayo, come little donkey come.
Me donkey fast, me donkey slow,
Me donkey come and me donkey go.
Me donkey fast, me donkey slow,
Me donkey come and me donkey go.

Happy Birthday to You

PAGE 4   MAY
MARIE: My birthday is May 10. I will have a party with
my friends. My mother will bake me a big, round cake.
PETER: OK. Let's play "Simon Says."

Simon Says Game
Simon says ..."put your right hand on your head"
                ..."touch the ground"
                ..."walk"
                ..."clap your hands"
                ..."say your name"
"Laugh out loud." "Simon didn't say!"

PAGE 5   JUNE
PETER: After Spring it is summer. In the summer we go
to the beach. I bring my beachball and toy boat.
MARIE: I bring my sand pail and shovel to the beach.
MARIE & PETER: We put on our swimsuits and build
huge castles in the sand.
MARIE: Medor, don't knock it down.

Row, Row, Row Your Boat
Row, row, row your boat
Gently down the stream
Merrily, merrily, merrily, merrily
Life is but a dream.

Sailing, Sailing
Sailing, sailing, over the bounding main
For many a stormy wind shall blow
'Til Jack comes home again.

A la claire Fontaine
This is a poetic French song about a girl walking in the
woods and singing about a lost boyfriend. She sings about
a beautiful fountain where they used to meet.

PAGE 6   JULY
MARIE: After we swim, we eat our picnic lunch. We eat
bread, cheese and bananas. It is delicious.
PETER: Oh no! Look at the ants.
MARIE: After our picnic, we go for a walk.

Day-O
Day-O, me say day-o,
        Daylight come and me wan' go home *repeat*
Work all night 'til the mornin' come,
        Daylight come and me wan' go home
Stack banana 'til the mornin' come,
        Daylight come and me wan' go home.
Come mister tallyman, tally me banana,
        Daylight come and me wan' go home *repeat*
Lift six hand, seven hand, eight hand bunch,
        Daylight come and me wan' go home *repeat*
CHORUS
A beautiful bunch of ripe banana,
        Daylight come and me wan' go home *repeat*
Lift six hand, seven hand, eight hand bunch,
        Daylight come and me wan' go home *repeat*
CHORUS
Words & music by Irving Burgie & Wm. Attaway.
Copyright 1955, renewed 1983. Cherry Lane Music
Publishing Co., Inc./Lord Burgess Music Publishing Co.
All rights reserved.

PAGE 7   AUGUST
MARIE: Today we go to the natural history museum.
PETER: It is my favorite place because there are so many
dinosaurs. Look at the triceratops. It has three points on
its head.

TRANSLATIONS

PAGE 8 AUGUST
MARIE: Next we go across the street to visit the art museum.
PETER: I like to look at the bulls in Goya's paintings. I pretend I am the matador.
MARIE: Look at the painting by Van Gogh. The sunflowers in his painting look like the ones in my garden.

Brown Girl in the Ring
Brown girl in the ring,
Tra-la-la-la-la *repeat*
She looks like a sugar
And a plum, plum, plum.

2. Show me a motion...
3. Skip across the ocean...
4. Do the locomotion...

PAGE 9 SEPTEMBER
MARIE: After summer it is autumn. The leaves turn gold and violet. I am gathering leaves and chestnuts.

Colchiques
This is a traditional French song about autumn.

PAGE 10 OCTOBER
PETER: Before we go back to school we visit grandpa's farm. We feed the cows, chickens and pigs.
MARIE: Grandpa shears the wool from the sheep. Later he takes us on a hayride with our cousins.

Down on Grandpa's Farm
Oh we're on our way, we're on our way
On our way to grandpa's farm *repeat*
Down on Grandpa's farm there is a big brown cow *repeat*
The cow she makes a sound like this: Moo! Moo! *repeat*

2. Down on grandpa's farm there is a little red hen.

Baa Baa Black Sheep
Baa baa black sheep have you any wool?
Yes sir, yes sir, three bags full.
One for my master and
One for my dame,
One for the little boy who lives down the lane.
Baa baa black sheep have you any wool?
Yes sir, yes sir three bags full.

Old MacDonald Had a Farm
Old MacDonald had a farm, E I E I O
And on his farm he had a cow, E I E I O
With a moo moo here, and a moo moo there
Here a moo, there a moo, everywhere a moo moo
Old MacDonald had a farm, E I E I O.
... had a chicken, cat, sheep.

PAGE 11 OCTOBER
MARIE: Today our parents take us to the harvest fair. The farmers bring their vegetables to be judged.
PETER: There are many rides for the children. I love to ride the merry-go-round.

PAGE 12 OCTOBER/NOVEMBER
PETER: It is Halloween. I am carving a face on my pumpkin.
MARIE: Tonight I will dress up in my Little Red Riding Hood costume and Medor will be the wolf. Peter will be a cowboy. Then we will go trick or treating with our friends. After Halloween it is November.

Five Little Pumpkins
Five little pumpkins sitting on a gate
First one said, "Oh my it's getting late."
Second one said, "There are witches in the air."
The third one said, "But we don't care."
The fourth one said, "Let's run and run and run."
The fifth one said, "I'm ready for some fun."
"Oo-oo," went the wind and out went the light
And the five little pumpkins rolled out of sight."

PAGE 13 DECEMBER
PETER: Look, snow is falling. Let us go and play in the snow. We take our sleds and slide down the hill.
MARIE: Then we build a snowman. He has coal eyes, a carrot nose and a derby hat. He wears my mother's scarf.

Silent Night
Silent night, holy night,
All is calm, all is bright.
'Round yon Virgin, Mother and Child,
Holy infant so tender and mild,
Sleep in heavenly peace.

Snowman Song
There's a friend of mine
You might know him too
Wears a derby hat
He's real cool.

He has coal black eyes
An orangy carrot nose
Two funny stick-like arms
And a snowy overcoat.

Have you guessed his name
Or do you need a clue?
You'll never see his face
In autumn, summer, spring.

PAGE 14 DECEMBER/JANUARY
MARIE: It is holiday time. We celebrate Christmas. We bake cookies and decorate our house. We sing special songs.
PETER: January first begins the new year. We have a party to celebrate on New Year's Eve.

Ce n'est qu'un au revoir, mes frères...
This is a traditional French song to the tune of Auld Lang Syne.

PAGE 15 FEBRUARY
MARIE: In February we celebrate the Mardi Gras carnival. It is fun . I like to catch candy at the parade. We sing and dance with our friends.
PETER: Now we know the months of the year. Do you?
JANUARY, FEBRUARY, MARCH, APRIL, MAY, JUNE, JULY, AUGUST, SEPTEMBER, OCTOBER, NOVEMBER, DECEMBER.

Good-bye!

Note: All efforts have been made to include literal translations.

NOTES

APPENDIX:
PRONUNCIATION KEY FOR FRENCH

THE FRENCH ALPHABET

FRENCH LETTER	HOW TO SAY THE LETTER	FRENCH LETTER	HOW TO SAY THE LETTER
Aa	ah	Nn	enne
Bb	bay	Oo	oh
Cc	say	Pp	pay
Dd	day	Qq	koo
Ee	uh	Rr	air
Ff	effe	Ss	esse
Gg	zhay	Tt	tay
Hh	ahsh, (usually silent)	Uu	oo
Ii	ee	Vv	vay
Jj	zhaa	Ww	doobluh vay
Kk	kah	Xx	eeks
Ll	elle	Yy	ee grek
Mm	emme	Zz	zed

CONSONANTS

The letter b, d, f, k, l, m, n, p, q and v have the same sound as English.
H is usually silent and w is pronounced as v.

FRENCH	PRONUNCIATION
c	before a, o, u, pronounced as *k* as in *kit* before e, i, and y, like the *s* as in *say*
ç	like *s* in *say*
ch	like *sh* in *she*
g	before e, i, y, pronounced as *g* in *sabatoge* before others, as *g* in *good*
gn	like *ni* in *opinion*
jo	zhaa, as *s* in *treasure*
r	as a slightly rolled *r*
s	usually like the English *s,* except between two vowels, like the English *z*
th	as *t* in the English language
t	the same as in English, except before ion, ieu, and ien, where it is like the English s
x	between two vowels, as ggs in eggs; elsewhere like s in *say*

VOWELS AND DIPHTHONGS

The French language uses additional markings, called accents, to give the vowel a different sound. Diphthongs are combinations of vowels that also create a new sound.

Vowels

FRENCH	PRONUNCIATION
a	like *a* in b*a*g
â	like *u* in b*u*g
e	like *e* in d*e*ck
é	like *a* in d*a*y
è, ê	like *e* in w*e*t
i, î	like *ee* in s*ee*
o	like *o* in h*o*me
u	like *ee* in f*ee*d
û	no equivalent in English; round lips for *oo* and try to pronounce *ee*
y	like a short *i* in Engl*i*sh

Diphthongs

FRENCH	PRONUNCIATION
ai, aî	between the *ai* in ch*ai*r and the *e* in r*e*st
an	between the vowels of *ah* and *oh*, with the n nasalized through the nose
au	like the *o* in *o*h
er	like *a* in d*a*y
ei	like *e* in w*e*t
eau	like *o* in n*o*
en	between *ah* and *oh*, with *n* nasalized through the nose
eu	like the *ea* in *ea*rth or *i* in s*i*r, pronounced with the lips pouted
ille	like *ey* in k*ey*
in	resembles the sound in *tan,* with the n nasalized through the nose
oe	like *earth,* pronounced with the lips pouted
oi, oî	like the *wa* in *wa*tch
on	between *ah* and *oh*, with the n nasalized through the nose
ou, ôu	like *oo* in n*oo*se
ui	like *wee* in w*ee*k

A B C D E F G H I J K L M N O P Q R S T U V W X Y Z

L'Alphabet Français

A — l'arc en ciel

B — le ballon

C — le camion

D — le dinosaure

E — les étoiles

F — les fleurs

G — la guitare

H — le hibou

I — l'insecte

J — le jardin

K — le klaxon

L — le lion

rainbow • balloon • truck • dinosaur • stars • flowers • guitar • owl • insect • garden • horn • lion • puppets •

M les marionnettes	**N** le nez	**O** l'ours en peluche	**P** le pain
Q la queue	**R** le réveil	**S** le soleil	**T** la tasse
U un	**V** la voiture	**W** le wagon	**X** le xylophone
	Y les yeux	**Z** le zèbre	

nose • teaddy bear • bread • tail • alarm clock • sun • cup • one • car • railway car • xylophone • eyes • zebra •

Vocabulaire du printemps
Spring Vocabulary
Find the matching words in the picture.

soil _____

strawberries _____

vegetables _____

pumpkin _____

apple seed _____

cabbage _____

tomato _____

garden _____

tulip _____

carrots _____

flowers _____

sunflower _____

grass _____

sun _____

Vocabulaire de l'été
Summer Vocabulary
Find the matching words in the picture.

clouds _____   cup _____

lake _____   thermos _____

beach _____   sunglasses _____

ant _____   swimsuit _____

sand _____   polo shirt _____

blanket _____   cheese _____

butterfly _____   banana _____

sailboat _____   picnic _____

waves _____   shoes _____

les feuilles
le ciel
les pommes
le tricot
l'oiseau
l'arbre
la veste
les châtaignes
le chat
le panier
la jupe
le chien
le pantalon
le râteau

l'automne

Vocabulaire de l'automne
Autumn Vocabulary
Find the matching words in the picture.

sky _____   apples _____

leaves _____   dog _____

knit sweater _____   jacket _____

cat _____   basket _____

skirt _____   pants _____

bird _____   tree _____

chestnuts _____   rake _____

Vocabulaire de l'hiver
Winter Vocabulary
Find the matching words in the picture.

hill _____

jacket _____

ice _____

snowflake _____

boots _____

cap _____

overcoat _____

sled _____

scarf _____

gloves _____

skates _____

snow _____

hat _____

eyes of coal _____

carrot _____

stick _____

snowman _____

ANSWER KEY TO SEASONS VOCABULARY WORDS

Le printemps (Spring)

le sol	soil	le jardin	garden
les fraises	strawberries	la tulipe	tulip
les légumes	vegetables	les carottes	carrots
le potiron	pumpkin	les fleurs	flowers
le pépin	apple seed	le tournesol	sunflower
le chou	cabbage	l'herbe	grass
la tomate	tomato	le soleil	sun

L'été (Summer)

les nuages	clouds	la tasse	cup
le lac	lake	le thermos	thermos
la plage	beach	les lunettes de soleil	sunglasses
la fourmi	ant	le maillot de bain	swimsuit
le sable	sand	le polo	polo shirt
la couverture	blanket	le fromage	cheese
le papillon	butterfly	la banane	banana
le bateau à voile	sailboat	le pique-nique	picnic
les flots	waves	les chaussures	shoes

L'automne (Autumn)

le ciel	sky	les pommes	apples
les feuilles	leaves	le chien	dog
le tricot	knit sweater	la veste	jacket
le chat	cat	le panier	basket
la jupe	skirt	le pantalon	pants
l'oiseau	bird	l'arbre	tree
les châtaignes	chestnuts	le râteau	rake

L'hiver (Winter)

la colline	hill	les gants	gloves
la veste	jacket	les patins	skates
la glace	ice	la neige	snow
le flocon de neige	snowflake	le chapeau	hat
les bottes	boots	les yeux de charbon	eyes of coal
le bonnet	cap	la carotte	carrot
le manteau	overcoat	le bâton	stick
la luge	sled	le bonhomme de neige	snowman
l' écharpe	scarf		